# Things We Used to Believe

Sam Foster

THINGS WE USED TO BELIEVE

Summersdale Publishers Ltd
46 West Street
Chichester
West Sussex
PO19 1RP
UK

www.summersdale.com

Printed and bound by Tien Wah Press, Singapore

ISBN: 1-84024-532-8
ISBN: 978-1-84024-532-5

# Things We Used to Believe

IF YOU SWALLOWED ORANGE PIPS AND DRANK
WATER AFTERWARDS, AN ORANGE TREE WOULD
GROW OUT OF YOUR HEAD.

IF YOU DIDN'T GO TO SLEEP BEFORE
NINE, YOUR EYES WOULD FALL OUT.

THE MOON WAS MADE OF CHEESE.

WHEN THE SUN SET, IT JUST WENT BEHIND A HILL. IF YOU WENT UP THE HILL, YOU COULD SEE IT RESTING.

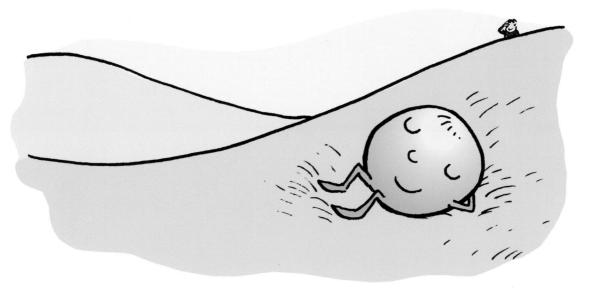

CATS WERE FEMALE AND DOGS WERE MALE.

IF YOU DIDN'T HAVE A CHIMNEY, SANTA COULD MAKE HIMSELF TINY AND COME IN THROUGH THE RADIATOR PIPES.

IF YOU WERE NAUGHTY, SANTA WOULD
BRING YOU COAL.

IF YOU RUBBED CHEESE ON A WART AND
BURIED THE CHEESE, THE WART WOULD GO AWAY.

IF A SPIDER CRAWLED INTO YOUR EARS
AT NIGHT IT COULD LAY EGGS, AND LITTLE
SPIDERS WOULD ONE DAY COME POURING OUT.

TELL LIES AND YOUR TONGUE WOULD TURN BLACK.

IF YOU PICKED A DANDELION YOU'D WET THE BED.

IF I ATE MY CRUSTS, MY HAIR WOULD GO CURLY. MY BIG SISTER ALWAYS LEFT HER CRUSTS AND HER HAIR WAS STRAIGHT.

IF YOU PULLED A FACE AND THE WIND CHANGED, YOUR FACE WOULD STAY THAT WAY.

THE WORLD WAS ALL IN BLACK AND WHITE IN THE OLD DAYS.

MY NEXT-DOOR NEIGHBOUR WAS CALLED
CHERRY BECAUSE SHE WORKED IN A CAKE SHOP.

THERE WAS A MOUSE LIVING IN THE MOON.
THIS MOUSE WAS NAMED LEON AND HE CAME
DOWN FROM OUTER SPACE, SAT ON MY
SHOULDER AND TALKED TO ME.

LEON.

PIRANHAS AND SHARKS LIVED IN THE WALLS
BEHIND THE POOL AND COULD COME ZIPPING
THROUGH THE FILTERS AT ANY TIME.

EATING POP ROCKS WITH COKE WOULD MAKE YOUR INSIDES EXPLODE.

GOD WAS A PAIR OF GOOGLY EYES FLOATING
IN THE SKY.

MY NEIGHBOUR'S CAT WAS A CREATURE FROM
OUTER SPACE, CONTROLLED INSIDE ITS HEAD
WITH LEVERS AND BUTTONS (LIKE THAT WEIRD
GUY IN THE NINJA TURTLES).

I WASN'T BORN BECAUSE I DON'T HAVE A BIRTHMARK. MY SISTER SAID I MUST HAVE BEEN MADE BY SOMEONE (LIKE AUNTY LINDA WHO TAUGHT TEXTILES) AND LEFT ON THE DOORSTEP, AND MAM AND DAD TOOK PITY ON ME.

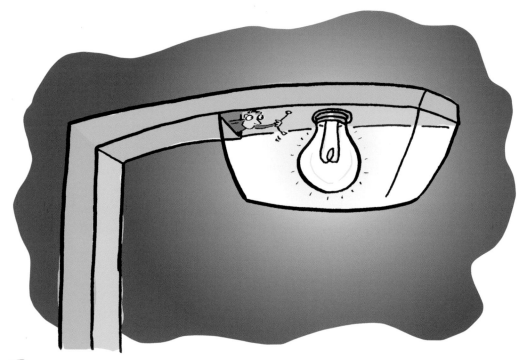

THERE WAS A TINY MAN WHO LIVED IN THE
LAMP POST AND TURNED THE LIGHT ON EVERY NIGHT.

RED CARS WENT FASTER.

IF YOU DUG A DEEP ENOUGH HOLE, YOU WOULD REACH AUSTRALIA.

I BELIEVED GIRLS BECAME BOYS WHEN THEY GOT OLDER, BECAUSE MY BROTHER WAS OLDER THAN ME.

a.　　b.　　c.　　d.

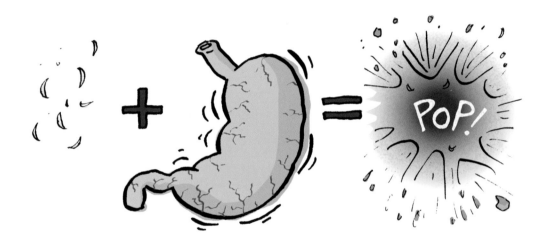

IF YOU BIT YOUR FINGERNAILS AND SWALLOWED
THE BITS THEN THEY'D POP YOUR STOMACH.

CHICKEN POX MEANT YOU WERE TURNING INTO
A CHICKEN. WHEN I GOT CHICKEN POX, I WENT
INTO THE GARDEN AND TRIED TO FLY BY
JUMPING OFF THE WALL AND FLAPPING MY ARMS.

IN PRIMARY SCHOOL, WE HAD TO PUT OUR HANDS UP TO ASK PERMISSION TO GO TO THE TOILET. THE TEACHERS CALLED THIS 'SPENDING A PENNY' AND WENT WITH US SO WE DIDN'T GET LOST. ONE DAY MY BROTHER STUCK UP HIS HAND AND THE TEACHER TOLD HIM THAT HE WAS BIG ENOUGH TO GO AND SPEND A PENNY BY HIMSELF. BUT HE COULDN'T WORK OUT WHERE IN THE TOILET THE PENNY SLOT WAS.

'BRITISH' MEANT 'MADE IN BRISTOL'. I WAS CHUFFED
TO BE LIVING IN THE MOST IMPORTANT CITY IN
ENGLAND. EVERYTHING SEEMED TO BE BRITISH.

I BELIEVED THAT A PARROT LIVED IN THE CUPBOARD IN MY PARENTS' ROOM. I WAS SHOCKED WHEN I OPENED THE CUPBOARD TO SHOW MY FRIEND THE PARROT, AND IT HAD DISAPPEARED.

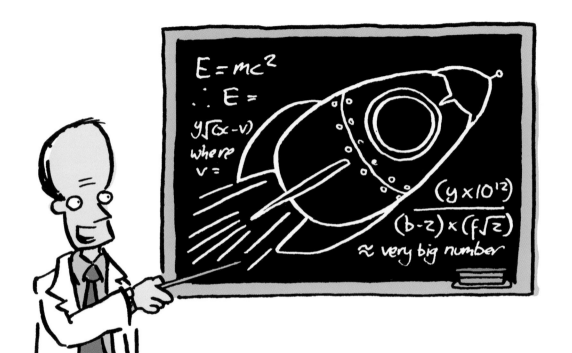

IF YOU HAD A BIG FOREHEAD,
YOU HAD A LARGER BRAIN.

IF THE TOE BESIDE YOUR BIG TOE
WAS LARGER, YOU'D BE RICH.

IF YOU SAT UPSIDE DOWN TOO LONG,
YOUR MEMORIES WOULD FALL OUT.

MY MUM TOLD ME WHEN WE MOVED TO ZIMBABWE I WOULD HAVE TO CROSS A ROPE BRIDGE SWINGING ABOVE A RIVER FILLED WITH RAVENOUS CROCODILES IN ORDER TO GET TO THE TOILET.

BROTHERS AND SISTERS HAD TO BE BORN ON THE SAME DAY OF THE MONTH.

I BELIEVED A FAMILY FRIEND LIVED IN THE BUS SHELTER. IF WE DROVE PAST THE BUS STOP AND HE WASN'T THERE, I'D THINK 'OH, CAMERON ISN'T IN TODAY.'

IF YOU PULLED A FUNNY FACE AND SOMEONE
HIT YOU ON THE BACK OF THE HEAD, IT WOULD
STICK FOREVER.

AS MY MUM KINDLY
ASKED ME IF I WOULD
LIKE A LITTLE BROTHER
OR SISTER, I BELIEVED
IT WAS DOWN TO ME
THAT MY LITTLE SISTER
CAME ALONG. WHEN SHE
GOT ON MY NERVES, I
USED TO TELL HER, 'I
WISH I'D NEVER
ASKED FOR YOU!'

I BELIEVED YOU SHOULD NEVER SCRATCH AN INSECT BITE BECAUSE THEY'D SPREAD. I SPENT MANY YEARS REPEATING THIS INFORMATION TO SCHOOL FRIENDS.

MY DAD TOLD ME THAT IF I BIT MY NAILS MY
ARMS WOULD FALL OFF, THEN MY LEGS WOULD
FALL OFF, THEN MY BODY WOULD FALL OFF AND
I'D BE JUST A HEAD. HE SAID HE KNEW A BOY
WHO WAS JUST A HEAD AND HE'D TAKE ME
TO SEE HIM SOME TIME.

I USED TO BELIEVE TRAFFIC LIGHTS WERE SCARED OF MY DAD. HE USED TO THREATEN THE LIGHTS TO MAKE THEM CHANGE FROM RED TO GREEN AND IT ALWAYS WORKED.

IF YOU WATCHED TOO MUCH TV, YOUR EYES WOULD GO SQUARE.

IF YOU CHEWED YOUR FINGERNAILS, YOU'D GET WORMS.

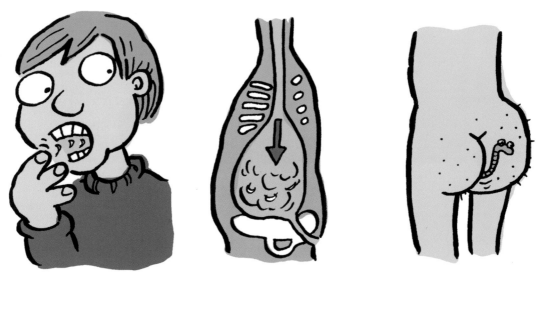

1.   2.   3.

THERE WAS A TATO (POTATO) MONSTER WHO LIVED IN YOUR TUMMY. TATO HAD TO GET FED AT LEAST ONCE A DAY WITH POTATOES — IF NOT, HE WOULD ESCAPE OUT OF YOUR MOUTH AT NIGHT AND EAT YOUR TOES INSTEAD.

IF I SWALLOWED CHEWING GUM, IT WOULD STICK MY INSIDES TOGETHER.

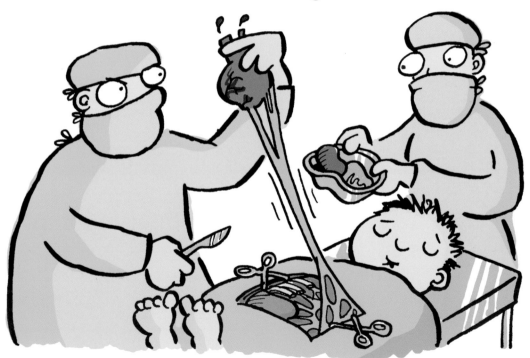

IF YOU SUCKED YOUR THUMB IT
WOULD TURN GREEN AND FALL OFF.

IF YOU WEREN'T IN BED ON CHRISTMAS EVE BY 8.00 PM, SANTA WOULDN'T STOP.

IF YOU PLANTED A PEACOCK'S FEATHER IN THE GARDEN, IT WOULD GROW INTO A BIRD.

IF YOU LOST SOMETHING, THAT WAS BAD, BECAUSE IF IT HAD GONE DOWN THE HOLE, YOU'D NEVER GET IT BACK — IT WAS GONE FOREVER.

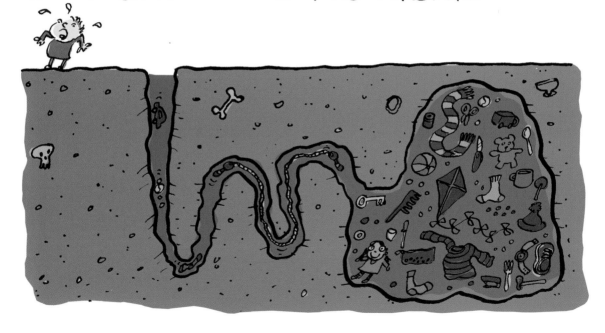

BAD FARM SMELLS WERE GOOD FOR YOU
BECAUSE THEY CLEANED OUT YOUR LUNGS.

'TO LET' SIGNS MEANT TOILET.

MY OLDER BROTHER TOLD ME THAT WHEN YOU GOT A BRUISE YOU COULD STOP THE PAIN BY PUSHING IT ALL OUT UNTIL IT STOPPED HURTING.

IF YOU PUT A TAPE RECORDER IN AN
AQUARIUM, YOU COULD HEAR THE FISH SPEAK.

BLACK COWS GAVE MILK AND BROWN COWS GAVE CHOCOLATE.

THERE WAS A LITTLE MAN INSIDE THE TV MAKING IT WORK.

YOU COULD SAIL TO JAPAN ON A RICE PAPER
BOAT WITH RICE PAPER SHEETS AND RICE PAPER
PLATES, AND THEN EAT IT ALL WHEN YOU ARRIVED.

SITTING WITH YOUR BACK TO THE FIRE
WOULD MAKE YOU SICK. I LATER FOUND OUT
THAT MUM SAID THIS SO WE WOULDN'T BLOCK
THE HEAT FROM GETTING TO HER.

IF I DIDN'T FINISH EACH AND EVERY KERNEL OF RICE FROM MY SUPPER BOWL, WHEN I GREW UP MY WIFE WOULD HAVE ZITS ON HER FACE.

MY GRANNY USED TO SAY, 'IF YOU PICK YOUR NOSE, YOUR HEAD WILL CAVE IN.' I WAS ON THE PARK AND RIDE IN CHESTER AND I SAW A MAN WHO HAD UNDERGONE MAJOR BRAIN SURGERY. HIS SKULL HAD A BIG DENT IN IT AND I FOUND IT HILARIOUS.

IF YOU SNEEZED AND FARTED AT THE SAME TIME, YOU'D TURN INSIDE OUT.

YOU COULD ONLY EAT ONE PEANUT AT A TIME OTHERWISE YOU'D CHOKE.

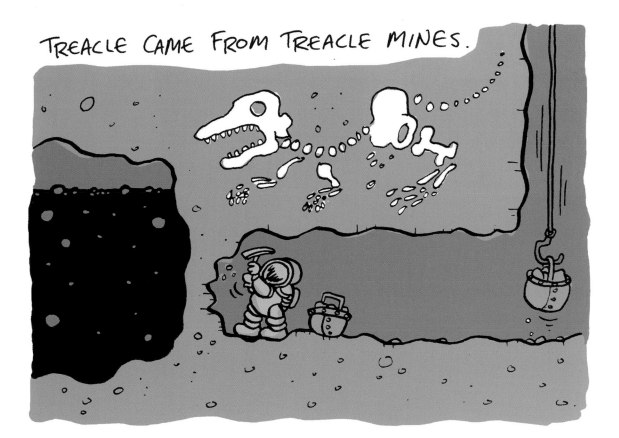

IF YOU HAD SEX BEFORE YOU GOT MARRIED,
ALL YOUR CHILDREN WOULD BE BATS.

IF SANTA FOUND YOU AWAKE ON CHRISTMAS EVE, HE WOULD EAT YOU. THAT'S WHY HE WAS SO FAT.

MY DAD TOLD ME THAT ICE CREAM CAME FROM ICE COWS. HE BACKED HIS POINT UP WITH THE FACT THAT I KNEW THERE WERE GRIZZLY BEARS AS WELL AS POLAR BEARS, AND I THOUGHT THAT MADE THE WHOLE ICE COW THING PRETTY PLAUSIBLE.

A MAGPIE WOULD COME AND BITE MY NOSE IF
I DIDN'T SAY 'GOOD MORNING MR MAGPIE.'

IF YOU PICKED YOUR NOSE,
YOUR FINGER WOULD GET STUCK.

WHEN I WATCHED THE SPOOF
FILM 'AIRPLANE' I BELIEVED
THAT THEIR PORTRAYAL OF
AN AUTOPILOT WAS WHAT
AUTOPILOTS WERE REALLY
LIKE IN REAL LIFE. I
WAS REALLY CONFUSED
AS TO HOW THE
BLOW-UP DOLL
THINGY
ACTUALLY
KNEW WHAT
TO DO!

ALL THE HAIR
YOU WOULD
EVER HAVE
WAS ALREADY
IN YOUR HEAD,
AND IT JUST
CAME OUT A
LITTLE AT A
TIME.

EVENTUALLY ALL TULIPS BECAME YELLOW ONES.

IF YOU DIDN'T LET YOUR
MOTHER TAKE OUT YOUR
SPLINTERS WITH A PIN,
THEY WOULD WORK
THEIR WAY INTO
YOUR BLOOD STREAM
AND TRAVEL UP TO
YOUR HEART AND
PIERCE YOUR
HEART, AND
THEN YOU
WOULD
DIE.

MUM SAID NOT TO LET GO OF MY SISTER'S HAND, OTHERWISE SHE WOULD FALL THROUGH THE CRACKS TO THE CENTRE OF THE EARTH.

I USED TO THINK THAT CURRENTS IN THE SEA WERE CURRANTS (AS IN THE DRIED FRUIT).

IT'S ALL FUN AND GAMES UNTIL SOMEONE LOSES AN EYE.

IF YOU WERE STRUCK BY LIGHTNING, YOU WOULD GET SUPERNATURAL POWERS.

UNICORNS WERE REAL.

EVERYTHING ON THE RADIO WAS LIVE. THE JACKSON FIVE WERE JUST IN THAT STUDIO SINGING THE SONG WE JUST HEARD, AND NOW THEY WERE RACING ACROSS TOWN TO GO SING IN ANOTHER STUDIO.

IF YOU ATE WATERMELON SEEDS, YOU'D GROW WATERMELONS INSIDE.

IF I COULDN'T SEE SOMEONE, THEY COULDN'T SEE ME, SO I COULD DISAPPEAR BY SHUTTING MY EYES. I DISCOVERED IT DIDN'T WORK AFTER MY DAD MIRACULOUSLY MANAGED TO FIND ME ONE DREADED BEDTIME STANDING IN THE MIDDLE OF THE LIVING ROOM EVEN THOUGH I HAD MY EYES COVERED.

# With thanks to

John-Paul Ahearne
Carol Baker
Jennifer Barclay
Arjun Basu
Michelle Berry
Barbel Brands
Natalie Butcher
Natalee Caple
Kate Chalk
Randy Chan
Julie Cheung-Inhin
Rachael Chivers
Bob Cripps

Sammy Cumes
Maria Cunningham
Nicky Douglas
Nicole du Preez
Lucy Farley
Kate Farmer
Martyn Farmer
Stewart Ferris
Alex Hallatt
Gillian Hennessy
Patrick Hinchey
Adele Kennedy

# With thanks to

Wendy Kerswill
Steph Little
Angela Mannion
Gavin Mills
Jenny Ng
Harriet O'Brien
Cleo Paskal
Joe Portelli
Jemma Rivers
Helen Roberts
Alyson Rudd
Charlie Sanger
Tamara Sheward

Rob Smith
Loraine Sommerfeld
Gill Soudsby
Katie Stewart
Murray Sutton
Trisha Telep
Jani Vrag
Trent Wilkie
Alastair Williams
Delyth Williams
Anna Wiseman
Lucy York

WWW.SUMMERSDALE.COM